D1376673

WILD AMERICA

RACCOON

By Lee Jacobs

BLACKBIRCH®
PRESS

THOMSON
★
GALE
™

San Diego • Detroit • New York • San Francisco • Cleveland • New Haven, Conn. • Waterville, Maine • London • Munich

THOMSON
━━━✦━━━
GALE

For
Lonnie
Pervos

For more information, contact
The Gale Group, Inc.
27500 Drake Rd.
Farmington Hills, MI 48331-3535
Or you can visit our Internet site at http: www.gale.com

Photo Credits: Cover, pages 5, 12, 15, 19, 20, 23 © Tom & Pat Leeson Nature Wildlife Photography; page 4 © Digital Stock; back cover, pages 3, 6, 7, 8, 10, 11, 14 © Corel; pages 8, 9, 16-17, 20 © PhotoDisc; pages 13, 22 © Thomas Kitchin & Victoria Hurst; page 18 © Art Today; page 21 © CORBIS

LIBRARY OF CONGRESS CATALOGING-IN-PUBLICATION DATA

Jacobs, Lee.
    Raccoon / by Lee Jacobs.
        p. cm. — (Wild America)
    Includes bibliographical references.
    Summary: Examines the raccoon's environment, anatomy, social life, mating, babies, and encounters with humans.
        ISBN 1-56711-644-2 (hardcover : alk. paper)
        1. Raccoons—Juvenile literature. [1. Raccoons.] I. Title. II. Series.
        QL737.C26 J33 2003
        599.76'32—dc21   2002002474

Printed in China
10 9 8 7 6 5 4 3 2 1

Contents

Introduction

The common raccoon is a frequent sight in backyards throughout North America. In Canada, they are found from Nova Scotia to British Columbia. Raccoons live all over the United States, except for some parts of the Great Basin Desert and the Rocky Mountains. More raccoons live in coastal areas than inland areas because they need a constant supply of water.

A related species, the crab-eating raccoon, lives in parts of Mexico, Central America, and northern parts of South America. This raccoon's body is slightly larger than the common raccoon's. Its fur is shorter and not as thick.

Raccoons are a common sight throughout most of North America.

Common raccoons and crab-eating raccoons both belong to the scientific family Procyonidae. Other family members include the coati, the kinkajou, and the cacomistle. The red panda was once included in the raccoon family, but scientists have now classified it in a different family.

The name raccoon came from the Algonquian Indian word "aroughcoune." It means "he scratches with his hands." These animals are well named. Common raccoons have nimble hands that they use almost as well as monkeys use theirs. Raccoons typically live for about 4 or 5 years, but some have been known to live for 10 to 12 years.

Raccoons belong to the same family as kinkajous (above left) and coatis (above right).

The Raccoon's Environment

Raccoons like to live near water.

Raccoons will live in nearly any place that has water. They love the water and are excellent swimmers. Raccoons make their homes in woodlands or near rivers, lakes, swamps, and marshes. They prefer to live in trees and search for hollowed-out trees or fallen logs. Raccoons are perfectly suited for climbing. They have sharp front and hind claws that help them grip things as they climb. Raccoons spend a lot of time high off the ground. Falling does not usually hurt them. A drop of 35 to 40 feet (11 to 12 m) won't bother a raccoon. They can even climb down a tree backward or forward, something most animals cannot do.

Top: Raccoons like to be high off the ground. **Above:** Raccoons sometimes hunt during the winter, but they store body fat to go without food if they have to.

Raccoons do not build their own dens. Sometimes they take over abandoned underground homes made by foxes, badgers, skunks, and other small animals. These burrows offer protection from predators (animals that hunt other animals for food) such as bobcats and great horned owls. Raccoons can also live comfortably alongside human communities. They find plenty of food where humans leave it behind. Raccoons are nocturnal animals. That means they are active at night and sleep during the day. They do not hibernate (sleep through the winter), but they will spend days or even weeks sleeping in their winter dens. Raccoons sometimes hunt for food in winter, but they don't need to. They store enough fat in their bodies to go without food during the winter months.

The Raccoon Body

The average adult raccoon weighs between 10 and 30 pounds (5 to 14 kg). A large male can weigh up to 45 pounds (21 kg). They are generally 9 to 12 inches (23 to 30 cm) tall. The length of an adult raccoon ranges from 18 to 28 inches (46 to 71 cm). A long, bushy tail adds another 8 to 12 inches (20 to 30 cm). A raccoon's tail is ringed with black. Most raccoon tails have between 5 and 7 rings.

Raccoons have small black noses, whiskers like those of a cat, and very sharp teeth. Their ears are pointed and have white tips and edges. Raccoons walk with a slight waddle because they have short legs and stocky bodies. The color of a raccoon's fur is usually gray or brown, except for the mask of black fur on its face. The mask is outlined in white.

Right (top and bottom): Ringed tails, catlike whiskers, and pointy ears are common raccoon traits.

The front paws of a raccoon are similar to a human hand.

Underbelly fur is usually lighter in color. As winter approaches, raccoons that live in colder areas develop a thicker coat to help keep them warm.

Raccoon tracks are easy to spot because a raccoon's front paws are much smaller than its back paws. The front paws are about 2 inches (5 cm) long, while the back paws are about 4 inches (10 cm) long. Raccoons have no fur on the palms of either the front or back paws. Their claws are not retractable. This means that their claws are always extended—they cannot pull them into their paws like a cat can. Raccoons are like humans in some ways. Raccoons have 5 distinct digits (fingers or toes) on their paws. And they walk flat-footed, as bears and humans do. Some raccoon tracks can almost look human. The tracks of a raccoon's front paws are similar in shape to a human hand. The back paws leave tracks that are shaped like small human feet with long toes.

Social Life

Most raccoons live alone.

Male raccoons mainly keep to themselves and live alone. Females also live alone, except when they are raising their young. Females and their babies live as a family group. After about a year, the young will go off to find their own places to live. Raccoons generally travel only as far as they need to find enough food. But a male will travel for miles when searching for a mate.

Although they like to live alone, raccoons do not guard their territory. A raccoon's home range is between 0.5 and 2 miles (0.8 to 3 km). This range often overlaps with the range of several other raccoons. Animals that live near each other often make a common area for leaving scat (droppings). These areas are called latrines.

Raccoons communicate with each other using a variety of different calls. If a raccoon is angry, afraid of something, or wants to warn another animal of approaching danger, it might make a barking, hissing, or snorting sound. These communication calls are important in a thick forest where one animal might not be able to see another. Raccoons may also purr when they are contented and whimper if they are injured.

Raccoons communicate with each other by using vocal calls and sounds.

Hunters and Raiders

Raccoons are classified as carnivores (meat-eaters) in the animal kingdom. But they are really omnivores, which means that they eat both animals and plants. Crayfish, rabbits, apples, grapes, frogs, snails, bird eggs, nuts, grasshoppers, caterpillars, corn, seeds, and even leftover hot dogs and hamburgers are all raccoon favorites. In fact, one of the reasons raccoons can live in so many different environments is that they eat so many different kinds of foods. And when their favorite foods are hard to find, a hungry raccoon will eat almost anything that offers some nutrition.

Raccoons will eat a wide variety of plants and animals.

Like all nocturnal animals, raccoons are most active at night.

Like other nocturnal animals, raccoons have excellent eyesight and hearing. This helps them find food in the dark. Raccoons use their expert hands to dig up clams, pick berries, catch fish, snatch eggs, and do many other things. They can even untie a rope, turn a doorknob, or open a refrigerator!

This page and opposite: Raccoons use their front paws to grasp food and hold it while it is inspected.

If there is water nearby, a raccoon may use its front paws to dip its food in the water a few times before eating it. People used to think that raccoons were washing their food. Scientists now believe that raccoons are using their hands to tear out parts of their catch that are not fit to eat. They do this mainly with food such as crayfish that they have captured in the water. But they sometimes do this with food they have found on land. Some scientists think this may be the raccoon version of "playing with your food."

The Mating Game

Raccoons only pair up when it is time to find a mate. Mating season for raccoons is between January and March. Most females are able to breed by the time they are 1 year old. Males are ready by 2 years of age. A female will only mate with one male in a mating season. But male raccoons mate with several females during each season. Most often, the male does not stay with the female for long after mating. However, some males will remain with the female for up to a week. Male raccoons do not help raise the babies once they are born.

Males and females usually pair up for mating between January and March.

Raising Kits

Pregnant females spend a lot of time resting in the winter. This prepares them for having babies in the spring. Female raccoons search for warm dens where they can settle in and be safe from predators. Sometimes a female will find an abandoned burrow made by a woodchuck or other small animal and move in. A female raccoon is pregnant for about 65 days before giving birth. The babies are called kits. Mother raccoons generally have a single litter per year of 4 or 5 babies. However, litters can be as small as 1 kit, or as large as 7.

Baby raccoons are born with their eyes closed—they only open about 21 days after birth.

The kits are tiny at birth—only about 4 inches (10 cm) long and weighing about 2 ounces (57 g) apiece. They are born with their eyes closed. Their eyes open at about 21 days of age. Kits are also born with a thin coat of fur. The black mask of fur on a kit's face is faint at first and darkens as the fur becomes thicker. The mother nurses her kits for about 16 weeks.

At first, the kits stay in the den with their mother. This protects them from predators such as owls, eagles, foxes, or coyotes. Newborn kits often sound like young birds when calling for their mother. Soon, the mother raccoon has to find a new home big enough for her growing babies.

She returns to the den to fetch them. Using her mouth, she picks each one up by the back of its neck and transports it to the family's new den.

Climbing and playing is an important part of a young raccoon's life.

Kits begin to walk between 4 and 6 weeks. By the time they are 2 months old, they can run and are learning to climb trees. They can also make a range of adult sounds such as alarm signals, fighting noises, and other communication calls. The kits are now ready to learn to hunt. They start to follow their mother out on hunting trips. Baby raccoons may stay with their mother for about a year before setting off to find their own territory.

Top and left: At about 2 months of age, kits are able to follow their mother out on hunting trips.

Young kits must learn to become expert climbers.

Raccoons and Humans

Natural predators of the raccoon, such as the bobcat, mountain lion, gray wolf, and coyote, are not found in many raccoon ranges anymore. But raccoons have much to fear from humans. Cars often kill raccoons. Raccoons were also killed for their pelts until about the 1930s, when raccoon fur went out of style. But raccoon hunting for sport is still popular in some parts of the United States.

Raccoons have learned to live close to humans. Often, however, humans consider raccoons to be pests.

The raccoon can make trouble for humans, too. Raccoons manage to get into most kinds of garbage cans—whether or not the can has a tight-fitting lid. Garbage-strewing raccoons have made many a mess in people's backyards! A female raccoon might move into someone's chimney to have her babies. If she does, however, she will not stay long. Soon, she will move her babies to a new location.

Raccoons have also been known to cause damage in cornfields, fruit orchards, gardens, chicken coops, and other places where people grow food. A field littered with half-eaten ears of corn is a sign to any farmer that raccoons are raiding the crop.

Many people also worry about getting rabies from raccoons. Rabies is a disease caused by a virus. It generally only infects wild animals. But a pet dog or a cat could get into a fight with an infected animal. If the rabid animal bit the pet, the pet could get the virus. People living in the eastern part of the United States were most afraid of rabies in the early 1990s. There was an outbreak and thousands of raccoons died. Today, this is less of a concern because most dogs and cats receive shots that protect them from rabies. There has also never been a reported case of a person getting rabies from a raccoon.

Although raccoons are commonly seen in backyards, it is important to remember that they are wild animals. They look cute and cuddly, but should be treated with the same respect as any other wild animal. It is best to leave them alone.

Glossary

carnivore animals that mainly eat meat

digit a finger or toe

hibernate to sleep through the winter

kit a baby raccoon

nocturnal an animal that sleeps during the day and is active at night

omnivore animals that eat plants and other animals

predator an animal that hunts another animals for food

retractable to draw something back in, such as claws

scat droppings

Further Reading

Books

Fowler, Alan. *Raccoons* (Rookie Read-About-Science). Chicago, IL: Childrens Press, 2000.

Merrick, Patrick. *Raccoons* (Naturebook). Chanhassen, MN: Child's World, 1999.

Nelson, Kristin L. *Clever Raccoons*. Minneapolis, MN: Lerner, 2000.

Swanson, Diane. *Welcome to the World of Raccoons*. Portland, OR: Graphic Arts Center Publishing, 1998.

Index